I0151822

Time in the Garden

Devorah Rubin

1st WORLD
PUBLISHING

Time in the Garden

Devorah Rubin

© Devorah Rubin 2006

Published by 1stWorld Publishing
1100 North 4th St. Fairfield, Iowa 52556
tel: 641-209-5000 • fax: 641-209-3001
web: www.1stworldpublishing.com

First Edition

LCCN: 2006937245
SoftCover ISBN: 978-1-59540-887-7
HardCover ISBN: 978-1-59540-888-4
eBook ISBN: 978-1-59540-889-1

This material has been written and published solely for educational purposes. The author and the publisher shall have neither liability or responsibility to any person or entity with respect to any loss, damage or injury caused or alleged to be caused directly or indirectly by the information contained in this book.

The characters and events described in this text are intended to entertain and teach rather than present an exact factual history of real people or events.

for Claire, Aissatou and Diane,
my best friends Judy, Jan, Mike, and Tracy—
all, women who inspired me to write

Contents

From the Garden

Souvenirs

Living Waters

About Time

.

From the Garden

our lives are lovely gardens
we were given at our birth

how we cultivate
these gardens
shapes our span of time
on this planet

※

as the bee
I would touch on life
and then
endue my tongue
with honey

Back to the Garden

What is this urge
that draws us back into the Garden?

The garden of our youth—
where every weed
was deemed a precious flower,
where buttercups and dandelions
were wove to garlands
braided in our hair.

The garden by the shore—
paved with paths of shells
around our castle walls;
groundscaped with weeds
culled from the sea,
lined with sprays of roses
picked along the way.

The garden of Day III—
when all was beauty,
pure and simple,
when roses had no thorns
and beasts pursued no prey,
before man woke
to see and use it.

In the Garden

Dayrise lights the morning sky,
silence soft enfolds the forest;
Shabbat *eyruv* link the trees; hung
banners stripe the quiet air;
　　　all is mine, I am alone.

Then purplejay comes into view,
hops to step and back to stone;
greycat prowls across my path,
purrs a greeting, and moves on;
blatant bird sits, nibbling cookies
　　　left abandoned on the stair.

Lamps glow darkly on the scene;
lights illumine empty rooms
where flagrant flags still shout SHABBAT
back to echoes, memories now.
It's Sunday morning in the Garden
　　　as it's seen by me, alone.

*An eyruv is a boundary around a Jewish community; at camp we
marked this boundary with colorful pennants*

Angels

There was a time
when I flew free
and called the universe
my home.

But then I thought
I'd like to try
to see and hear
and think a while.
I traded in
that vast eternal space
to spend some time
in this small mundane place.

On special nights
I set my altar,
kindle lights, and
make my prayers,

summon in the
holy messengers
to join me here in this,
my earth-bound journey.

My Garden

I'll take the snips
    and leavings of my life
        and make a mulch of them,
and when I'm there
    and ready,
        grow a garden—
like the deep forest grows
    where there is space
        accidents of beauty,
wild and wonderful—
    to brighten,
        draw the sun.

Tiger lilies,
    gold and honey
        shot with light,
bloodroot, white eyes glowing
    from dark and barky roots
        and leather leaves,
wild rose, spilling
    pale and scentless
        over rocks and craggy places.

I'll grow my garden—
    lilies, roots, and roses—
        choose my spot,
draw the light,
    and give it back,
        a splash of color.

Cactus Flower

I watched a child grow
lovely, straight and strong,
a brilliant mind and restless soul,
intelligence unmixed with understanding
knows no peace.

Imagine then, a stunted desolate place,
all rocks and crags, sand and stones,
where twisted shapes of shadow
try to grow to shade
to save the bitter store of water
deep within their core.

I had a bright and lovely child;
when she begged discipline,
why could I not
have led her first with love?

Do you blame the cactus for its spiny
scentless growth, or bless it for
its occasional sweet flower?

Polyantha

There is one who's gentle
        and likes the special things
   of art and beauty.

The wild rose of my life,
       soft tender petals
   quiet and unscented
       there to light her corner.

Her roots go deep
       into the masonry of her wall
   and form a patterned crack
       across the bricks
  to give her sustenance
       and space to grow.

Once she has her map or key
       to the basic sense of order
   deep within her being,
       she'll have a lever
  strong enough to move the universe,
       a galaxy, her own imprisoned self.

Ode to Michal

Small earth woman
    —Astarte, Amazon combined—
soft female form,
      all wound in working muscle.

Delphic daughter
    —Pipes of Pan and angled dance—
unbound hair and flowing silk,
      weaving patterns in a forest dell.

Smiles and sparkle
    —fun and laughter—
soon replaced with sounding horn
      and the Legion's battle dress.

Butterfly

I had a touching child,
the kiss of a butterfly's wing,
pure and beautiful—so young.

What did I do,
where did she go?
She is grown,
her color's gone from lovely
loved and loving lavender
to nature's wild magenta.

The good is there;
bring back the sweetness
and her loving nature
will do the rest;
bring back the peace
she needs to glow and grow
and calm her outer shell;
rearrange the borders of her days,
surround her with a harmony
she may reflect;

show her the image
she will want for her own
good—*Tovah.*

My Anchor

He is the anchor
to my soul.

When I stand at the threshold, drying
my wings in the flowing light
he calls me back—
what are you doing?
—nothing!

When I'm at rest unfolding as a flower,
my layered petals,
he stays me with a touch—
what are you doing?
—nothing!

When I am testing
the depths of my being,
ready to immerse in
the full tide of truth,
he calls me back, enfolds me—
what are you thinking now?
—nothing!

Strange, like the covenant
I wear around my neck,
his name means life—*Chaim.*

Tapestry

When the time has come for me to rest
I hope that I can truly say
I have accomplished all that was
    intended that I do;
    if not, I'll surely hope to say
    I've tried.

The petty tasks, the daily chores
bleed off the hours
of my life's allotment.
    To do the things I must, in time allowed—
    I would abjure the menial duties so I may
    complete the larger tasks I'd settle for.

A tapestry—of necessity,
quick-wove with vibrant colors
and strong thread—
    leaves no time for petit point
    in variegated shades of silk
    to give it depth.

Growth

The seasons turn
the earth moves along
its journey through
the stations of the sun.

Time has brought me friends
from unexpected places;
bring them to my garden now
and let me dream on them.

The *Cactus Flower* blooms
in her sun-drenched home,
surrounded by a love
that overflows,
encompasses her world.

My *English Rose*
has grown from
shy and scentless polyantha,
to full bloom, confident to
shape her own domain.

The *Earth Woman*, my amazon
now marches to a muted drum;
she sings a sweeter song
and fills her world
with music.

And my lovely *Butterfly*,
grown from magenta
to a splash of purple,
flits from nest to busy-ness
content and happy
in her world.

About Prayer

when I'm drawn
to a sunny spot,
see a rusty lizard
on an Arizona rock,
I know God played
with the colors brick and clay...

a spotted snake,
merged with sandy soil,
tells me ten shades of tan
were blended on the palette...

a feather fanned to form
the pattern of a spiny leaf
is a planned event...

a blossom moved
to show itself
a butterfly on wing
is a message
from the Creator...
and that is prayer...

when I'm at high places
on a cliff
looking out to the ocean
or a ridge
at the top of a mountain
I know spiritual peace...

as birds who gather—
in the highest branches
of the tallest trees—
to greet the dawn,
when the sun
finds my spot—I fly—
weaving songs of praise...
    and that is prayer...
Amen

Stratum

When I tell your daughter
of the you that lived with me—
    we speak of moments
    that stand clear and
    feelings that run deep.

Tonight we fold back
the layers of your life,
meet the fiercely independent
child you would become—
    and I watch you form your
    friendships, one by one.

We share your happy journeys,
laugh at papers that you wrote—
    I picture you again
    playing scales at 5 a.m.

As we read your essays,
marvel at the load of work you kept—
    I see you taking honors
    in a long white borrowed dress.

When we pack away
your notebooks—
    I journey back to Westconn
    stand again outside your room,
    embrace once more the woman
    working at her desk.

We share your photo albums
but the pictures that I keep
will stay with me, inside me—
        of you stepping through the door, then
        calmly, firmly, planting roots
        in that distant desert home.

When I speak now to your daughter,
and tell her of the you I knew,
her eyes go wide with wonder
at this other view of you.

Regarding Weeds

Daisies were Tracy's choice
weeds that they are;
my memory of her on a hillside
surrounded with their brightness
is as strong
as their hardy stems.

Yarrow grows tall and serves
as accents in the garden;
when I bought one for mine
Janice was amused,
Mom, it's just a weed!

Where rosemary thrives
a woman rules,
is *Wiccan* knowledge;
each time I've put it
in my garden,
my husband pulls it up for weeds.

We're warned *strew rue,*
and you will rue the day.
I see promise in its buds
and softness in its leaves
and beauty in the hint of blue
that glows through
all the green of it.

I'd marry it to lavender
in my garden and my plot.

When I admired flowers
in her bouquet, Jan laughed.
The purslane was food
plucked from the path
between the peppers,
the chickweed was a diet aid
and not an eyesore to be destroyed,
parsley's such a vibrant green
and tastier than fern, and
goldenrod's blurred yellow
just blended with the rest.

Music, Body and Soul

Mike's at *The Planet*, 5 a.m.
rough aerobic music pounds:
Move that Body, make it burn,
count, in cadence, sets to ten,
move along the circuit, start again.
Go, go, go—nautilus and weights,
sweat and strain, and work it out.

With the *Bristol Brass*, Michal
measures hours, note-by-note,
Mozart, Brahms, and Bach.
The *Ode to Joy* is followed
by degrees of *The Messiah*
lofting, phrase-by-phrase, in
increments to the set patterns
devised by Masters of the Meter.

While she works
Soduko puzzles on her stool
at the *Rendezvous Bar*,
her soul soaks up
the fiddle and the low growl
of someone's unrequited love.
Then a break for lines and squares
and *Texas Two Step*; keep it close
let the music spin you round
entwine you in a parody
of shared and breathless rapture.

Working the Dig

Three ceramic gulls perched on
their pile of cork beside a plastic ocean,
wait to go to flight with just a touch
to set them into simulated motion.
Tracy got them in '70 when she was 6
on a trip with Aunt Jeanette at Mystic.

Now this mirrored music box
sits silent, gone the magnetic butterfly,
and flown, now, is my Butterfly.
Her sisters gave her that when she was 10,
a fine joke 'til she played it days on end.

An old carved trinket box
holds a broken chain, and
a beaded baby bracelet
that spelled out her name.
She got that at thirteen, along with money,
and left them behind when she was 20.

This lovely princess gown
in vibrant yellow,
was altered twice, and so
there's no one left that it would fit.
She wore it once in '81 and once again in '82.

And here's her old recorder
and a box of music that she used,
graded cards and college records,
and a W2 that's dated '84.

Ah, here's my box
of yarn and needles;
let's find some variegated
pink and blue;
get my fingers busy
my baby's due to have a child
now, in two thousand one.

Little Bird

I watch you as your sleep,
wonder at the life of you.
Do you think and do you dream;
are you just content to grow?

Sad, that I won't see you so
another year from now;
you, small bundle curled,
safely tucked so close.

You'll grow, as children do,
change will come as changes must;
you'll stretch your frame,
expand to fill your space.

As every mother did and will,
I'll forget the curl of you
and see instead the you
that you become.

The Kiss

White crocus bloomed
in my front garden
on the day Renee
formed her first kiss.

First sign of growth
and spring
promise of the wonders
time will bring.

Will this fleet touch
of lip on cheek
seem sweet to her
as it does to me?

Will it be as fixed
in memory
as the beat of wings
in years long past
when lashes flipped
soft on my face
as my *Butterfly*
first kissed me?

Grandma's Garden

First, we check the angel in the tree,
count the blue forget-me-nots
one by one; when we're done
see if 'nancy' polished
all her pretty leaves for me.

Tulips stand up tall,
Grandma tells me, *smell*—
and when I stick my nose in
bright red tulip cups,
their eyes are winking back at me.

There's my 'April valentine',
each branch is hung with hearts
that say *please be mine*;
if I look close around
the bigger flowers' feet
I see the purple pansies
turning faces to the sun.

Her other garden's only leaves;
some will be: coral-bells
to call the fairies out to play;
bergamot to bring the butterflies;
and tickseed's yellow stars attract the bees.

My Grandma tells me look
and smell, but mustn't pick.
This garden's here for me—
last year when I was three—
and next year when I am five—
it will be back again to see.

Tomorrow we'll plant some
dusty millers with my little scoop.
Next week when I come back
we'll do some 'patience' plants
and put the perky pink petunias in.
Grandma's garden's lots of fun
and such a pretty place to be.

If I were Single

would I keep
a six-room Cape for just
two rooms to eat and sleep;
and would I use
that other space
for so much stuff
that needs a place?

Single,
would I cook for one
or would I eat out just for fun;
would a tea date
take the place of
a hum drum meal
in the marriage race?

Single
would I settle for a cat
for a companion?
Yes, I'd do it, just like that.

If I were single
all these years
would I have laughter
more than tears;
would I read more books,
and make more rhymes,
and sew more quilts,
and have more time—to live?

On Being Me

Who am I, and
    what am I doing;
where have I been,
    and where am I going?

Mother, sister, wife and friend;
    sharing, caring, full of past;
all the years that make me, *me*
    come to surface, used at last.

Rules I gathered back in school,
    places, near and far, I've known;
pages out of photo albums,
    people, filed away, who've flown.

All these are the essence of
    the *me* who knows the way to live
the moments of each passing day
    with cherished memories.

The Aran Diamond

the words in italics are cable pattern stitches

my ballet in ninety-three stitches
bend and twist,
turn, jete, passant
cable needle set to go

working through the *Diamond*—
now, a field of *wheat*
plump and heavy
ready for the reaping

and the rows of *trinity*
become a patch
of *blackberries*
full of promise

there, the skein of *gulls*
wide wings beating
flying high and free
above the
strong massed *cables*.

All these panels
worked for marriage beds
and smaller covers,
bordered, for the babies' cribs.

Aran Diamonds
cross the Continent
west to California
north to Oregon and south
to Baltimore and Georgia
the single tie my
nimble fingers
dancing their ballet.

Ebony and Ivory

When I was young, I played with COLORED KIDS,
older, I had some NEGRO friends.
As a young woman, I knew AFRICAN AMERICANS
who would be at loss to show a visa.

Today they're BLACK—but no more
BLACK than I am WHITE;
some, mahogany perhaps
as Aissatou is, or chestnut
with an undertone of rose
like my young friend Ch'Toya.

Cindy's honey maple, with
a golden glow that I admire.
My skin is buff, and when I blush
it has a touch of pink;
it's dry red when I've had too much sun,
and mottled sepia's as close
as I can come to tan.

Friends

I know you.

I know the pattern of your hand,
    and the look behind your face
        that never changes.

In this life
    so many friends have come to me
        and then gone on their way,
    as brightly colored blossoms pass
        once they have had their day.

I bless the moment
    of the meeting, the spark that
        touched my soul and made it sing.

Welcome to my world,
    my friend, and now—
        goodbye.

In Reflection

Let my mirror image be
one of peace and tranquility.

Let no one say I gave her back
a scene of heavy, dark or muddy hues.

Let the picture I leave on your mind be
a serene glow, a bright and loving light.

When my children see me,
may they see—warmth and love.

When my friends see me,
may they see—bright interest,
time to share.

Today

Today I saw you cross the street
your sandaled feet were swift,
your skirt swung with a purpose,
the nimbus of your ungrayed hair
still framed your lovely face.
I turned and called your name,
quick retraced my steps;
I looked where I had seen you go
down Shipyard Lane
around the corner out of sight
but—you were gone.

Last month I thought
I heard your voice
carried strong across a room;
when I looked into the crowd
I could not find you—
you were gone.

Last week I watched a sun set,
blaze of glory, on your pond;
I thought to share the view
turned to talk to you
but—you were gone.

Time in the Garden

This happens
with close friends
and to the new bereaved;
but it's been years—
since you've been gone.

Almanac

There is a season for each thing in life,
        and when its time is due, somehow
    we find the strength and purpose of the task.

When time is come to build a tower,
        we find stones, and when it's time
    to plant our garden, seeds.
If we try to plant at tower time
        the ground holds firm and shovels break,
    and muscles are not equal to the chore.

Like fish, we find our time to swim;
        like birds, we're given
    paths that we must fly.

Once learned, our life's design
        is a clear mosaic, there to read
    with our eternal inner eye.

The schedule of our years
        reads like an almanac
    that sets the wheeling pattern of our days.

Vernal Equinox

Nature's golden finger,
        warmed by the sun,
    now sets its living touch on
        winter's hard and brittle scene.

The sere lines blur
        as branches stretch
    and buds swell full and ready
        to release a new year's bloom.

A day of sun to urge its growth,
        a day of dark and rain to nourish it,
    and one more frost to test
        the new crop's strength.

It's almost spring;
        and life, once furled,
    cannot return
        to bud's tight womb.

As every gardener knows,
        his choice is clear,
    the cultivated plant
        has less of seed and scent.

Seeds planted early,
        given little care,
    will flower to hardy
        more abundant plants;

the blossoms, though much smaller,
            are more generous in number—
      their heady scent sends forth
            a loving welcome to the world.

Reprise

Fold back the pages
    of my life and find
        the book-marked day,
one gold en-
    capsuled afternoon
        warmed by the sun.

Now bring it back complete,
    the smell of lilac
        and the hum of bees;
hear, in the distance,
    sleepy chirps as birds
        shift in their trees.

Stitch it all with dragonflies'
    stiff emerald wings
        that catch on every breeze,
make a closure
    of your self and
        fold it round that scene.

Loose persistent winter's grasp
    with that one warm amber moment
        of a single summer's day.

Views of Fall

A branch of red
atop the deep full green,
harbinger of fall
along the highway.

Next trip up the Merritt—
brilliant gumdrops,
nested row on row
in their bon-bon box
high up on the hill,
catch my eye.

For forty years, I loved
the bright maples
across the street,
last to bud and bloom
and last to flame and fade,
that filled the canvas
of my parlor window.

Then my friend died
and Amy moved in—
I don't need trees, she said . . .and now
my window's empty,
bare, nothing there
to mark the seasons,
satisfy my soul.

Reflection

There is a moment on a winter's day
when all the earth is frozen fast
encased within a looking glass
of ice.

Look through the one-way mirror,
frame our summer garden now,
set it in its place, and dream on it.

Remember all the love we'll want to see
and leave behind.
Remember now the order and the plan
we'll need to make our space secure.
Remember as it is planted it will grow.

We think we'll plant and prune
and then transplant again
when all the garden's there.

Sometimes the seedlings won't be moved
and there's a plant that's lost
and balance in the garden, gone.
Sometimes the season's too far gone
when next we look, and to our vast dismay
our garden will not let itself be changed.
Sometimes the gardener's gone
and garden's all that will remain,
intact and private as a signature.

She'kinah

Blessing the wine, spice, and candle of Havdalah

In the wide meadow, surrounded by silence,
still wrapped with *she'kinah*
look to the heavens, count the stars
draw together in our circles,
as we sway and softly sing
the haunting melody:
> *yai, la, lai, lai, lai, lah...*

Gather close this one more time
in love and everlasting peace
as we end our sojourn in the Garden.

Boruch attah...
bless once more the sweet elixir.
Boruch attah...
share again the warmth and light of *Shabbat*.
Boruch attah...
hold close the spiced fragrance of the day.

Now trailing *she'kinah*, sweet spirit, to sustain us,
call Eliahu as our witness, wish our friends
the goodness of the week to come
Shavuah Tov, Shavuah Tov.

Souvenirs

celestial events
scenes of wonder
memories I've brought back
from places I've been—
these are my souvenirs

Aquarius

The world has waited long
for its new age.

The stars wheel and wait
the constellations pace
through their eternal path.

One day we'll join them
and in glory be
all that we were meant to be.

Peace, love, and harmony
these three can move
the universe.

The universe, I think,
is ready to be moved
and so am I.

Kensington Gardens

I follow your medallions
bronze compass points at every junction;
a pilgrim
down the *Flower Walk,*
rampant with a tapestry of color
exotic blooms brought from
your global journeys;
past the maze of quiet trees;
soft waving grasses
tease my eye with glimpses of the pond.
I look for you
on every turn
in all your favored vistas.
Your hand is there
your spirit lives
though you are gone.

I shadow you past
the *Children's Park*
where toddlers reign
and adults are attendant;
round the *Serpentine Gallery*
devoted to the nouveau art you loved;
cross Baywater Street,
dodging traffic as you did,
to your Café;

it bears your name
its decor, floor to ceiling,
imaged you in every aspect,
a shrine to the beloved Di.
>   *Diana came here often;*
>   *she's gone, we miss her.*

I walk your paths
in my mind, my heart;
see Diana's Fountain
with my eyes,
the rush, the splash over
concrete jumps to the left,
the flowing ripple down
the cement diamonds to the right;
here, where I stand,
a still quiet pool
like you
at rest, at rest.

Metamorphosis

When I wear black
I'm tall and slender
my hair feels right
my eyes are bright
and all the world's
my runway to the stars.

In Alice blue
I'm short
and dull
my hair's too straight
the day is one
I feel a frump.

I don't wear red
by choice
sometimes it just
occurs—the blacks
are in the wash and
nothing else will
button at my waist.

But when I wear my
purple silk
with those special
red-toned slacks,
the crimson hat
and the paisley scarf
in the style the Tajikistan
at Liberty's in London
taught me—
I am audacious.

Signage

If you think to do it—Don't

Mind the Gap,
on bumper stickers and gimme caps,
and in the Tube:
Clear the doors,
Move left, Stand right.
Clear the doors, count to ten
before they slam them shut again.
Move right within the doors,
make room for others.

At every corner:
Look Left, where every sense
tells you the cars come from the right,
and then: *Look Right,* too late
my eye's still trained to left.

Mind your bags everywhere you go.
Ladies Toilets with the hours
engraved in bronze and an addendum:
Dogs are not admitted.
Post boxes for: *Dog Waste,*
put your litter in your pocket.

This old culture's
learned its lesson well:
Don't wait until the deed is done
to punish. Best to warn off
while it is still a seed of thought—
a twinkle in a naughty eye.

Random Birds

I've never heard a raven's song. I've watched
proud peacocks as they trod
the grounds at Scone in Scotland,
their orb'd tails spread wide in welcome
to the guests who came to wonder at
their grandeur.

The peacocks perched atop the roof
of the summer stage, at Beardsley Park,
were known to trill along with
Irish tenor's songs that struck
their fancy.

I found more than little brown birds at the
station on the deck in Rocky Hill:
hooded juncos, tiny tufted titmice,
copper-feathered winter finch and
messy-eater chickadees lined up
at the squirrel-proof feeder.

The purple jay amazed me
hopping down the morning path,
at a camp ground in Santa Rosa,
to nibble breakfast from an
abandoned cookie.

In Kentucky I watched in awe as
the skunk bird, with his broad white stripe
swooped heavy across the lawn,
straddled the rotten hickory,
peck, pecking as he searched
for grubs for breakfast.

There's such a beauty to a bird
from beak to flipping tail,
I wonder that I've gone so long
through life not noticing
their splendor.

Wednesday's Child

One year I went to visit
Center Church, there in the middle
of our nine-block green.

Up on the wall of that old church
were lists of folk who'd lived, and died,
when this was just a harbor town.

Their graves, first laid in meadows
mowed by grazing sheep, now moved
into the Center's stony crypt.

We found whole families
gathered there—husbands
and their several wives,
mothers and their broods.

Laid low by sickness and disease,
they'd been taken, each in turn,
until whole clans had disappeared.

There's one I'll not forget,
her name was Sarah Ann, born
eight years before she died on April 31!

Was she the last of April's jokes
or were they loath to say
she died the 1st of May

when other children gave
sweet violets and
pansies to their mom?

This mother's only flowers
were the ones she laid upon
her daughter's winding sheets

to keep her fresh, till
they laid her to rest in
her last and lonely bed.

In Another Garden

Jessica's baby, Megan Marie—so quiet
in her picket crib with angels at her head and feet
to guard her while she sleeps.
Two lamps to keep the night at bay
and lambs and dolls to make her smile
if she should wake.

So many other babies born one day
and gone within a week.

Jessie and one son who made the journey
on a fateful day in April, Ruben
followed them too soon, on November 22.

Claude has bunnies on his bed,
the picture at his head shows him with
Rover and his favorite gun
at sunrise in an open field.
He was a loner first to last
but seems he left a lot of friends.

There's Jessie and Grace, the patriarch
and matriarch, and back of them
their family Ansel, Clare, and Estil
with their spouses named.
All, born at random dates and left
in the decade before 2000 with
no clue to why and how they went.

It's quiet now at Privett Field;
no one to answer questions,
no one to tell the story of these folk;
no sign of who's been there to plant
the plastic flowers, light the lamps,
and say the evening prayers.

Solar Eclipse

Don't think now
of what this small moon
can accomplish
when it mounts
its regular invasion
on the awesome face
of our distant sun.

Leave logic loose and lame
while we watch
celestial bodies
play their hiding game.
A nibble, then
a chomping bite,
and half a world
is gone to starry night.

Worship

Imagine the time when
the first man looked up
into the leaves of the first tree
and thought he saw the sun
caught fast in its twiggy web.

Imagine the night when
the first woman watched
the moon, move through its
stations in the sky, and thought
it laid itself to rest.

Imagine now the day
they watched as the sun
was swallowed by the moon,
and saw attendant stars rush to
that corner of the sky!

Imagine then
that is when
they first
learned how
to pray.

Night Wonder

At three a.m., I watched in awe
as god unzipped the sky.
One and another light splashed out,
the Dipper filled again;
I saw a long scream rend its way
across the Night Star's path.
Orion split, but stood his ground
and kept his sword held high;
The Bull just kept on lumbering,
and Cassi's veil held fast.

What did we think so long ago
when Leonis did this—
and spilled his stars across the sky
like sand across the strand?

Were we anxious for the constancy
of patterns that we knew;
did we worry that the morrow
would have a sky all new
with pictures and with stories un-
familiar to our view?

Did we fear we'd lose our compass
to orient the sky
and have to find another North
to reckon journeys by?

Storm

Cloud on cloud on cloud
sky is heavy, dull
begging for release
trees stand tall
twiggy fingers turn
to touch the laden air
    storm is coming.

Sky like molten glass
the day turns brass
birds sit puffed and silent
geese gauble
wend their way
away from water
    storm is coming.

Sky's as restless as the sea
waves of clouds
move silent on a liquid shore
trees twist and tangle
dance to gusty music, then
hang heavy, dark, unmoving
    storm is coming.

Pressure's up, my ear
sings in rhythm with the wind
all my being longs to fly
my feet are anchored fast
while currents
toss and swirl
 the storm is come.

The Legacy

The blizzard they called Daniel
came in on Sunday night;
the fine farina fall of snow
came down an inch an hour,
drifted high and fell again.
All day Monday,
we shoveled fast and
swept it clean away, but
Daniel wasn't finished yet.
Some wind, more snow;
then, on Tuesday
we had to dig it all again.
Now it measured five feet high;
the sun shone down, cold and
bright, on snow piled high
around each isolated house.
Wednesday, we discovered
ice—on streets and walks, and
packed in all our drains and
gutters, solid as a cork.
The next day we were tested
with Storm Daniel's parting shot:
a February Thaw!
The heat went up by one degree
for each of thirty hours.
Five feet of snow packed down to four—

and four compressed to three.
The drains broke free
and icy flow poured down
to meet the melting snow
then puddled all the streets
and low dug cellars;
we lost our power
—for just a little while—
and it returned with such a force
it set the clocks all back to twelve
and turned electronic drones
to blinking fools!

The clocks are back,
radio and TVs the same,
the microwave's ok,
the fridge and stove are fine, but

my AOL has bit the dust,
my Gateway's closed,
the files are locked up fast
deep in the Tower's keep;
Heavens, Daniel, what did you do?
You fried my motherboard!

Devorah's Astral Journey

Ursa Minor RH35h 5m 52s

I've a passport to paradise,
a key to the cosmos,
my very own place
in the reaches of the sky.
Polaris shares my portion,
gives me a ready constant
to set my compass by.

Start at the North Star,
travel south along the handle
through the ladle to the lip;
there, in that spill of stars,
you'll find the one that
bears my name.

Have I ever wandered there
somewhere back
on the other side of time;
or, will I go there yet when
this day's journey's done;
and if I do, will I know
to call it home?

Living Waters

the life force
that binds us one to another
the spiritual stream
that flows between us
the soothing power
of the sea:
they are
precious gifts

The Mikvah

Stripped to my skin
my outer self bared
naked as the dawn
unshelled and quivering
I step out to meet my fate.

Rose is there to guide me;
though she never touches me
I feel her fingers on my face,
in my hair, across my shoulders,
down my body to my toes.

> *No jewelry, hairpins, earrings?*
> *You don't wear contacts?*
> *Nothing in your mouth?*

The door's ajar,
my *Bet Din* on the other side,
to hear me take my test.
There's only Rose and me
and somewhere—God—
and all around, the hollow echo
of the empty pool.

> *OK, immerse, step in.*

Down the steps
the heavy water swirls
past my hips, my waist, my breast;
one deep breath...
I'm in! I'm down ... and up!
    You'll have to try again;
    your hair is long, it floats.

Down I went again,
sat on the bottom of the pool
to count my time to ten,
then up... *Boruch attah...*
then again...*Boruch attah...*
and then, *Amen.*
Somewhere in that time
the Marilyn I was is gone
Devorah has moved in
I am a Jew.

Connections

Ah blessed release
the burden eased
that's kept me
heavy, slowed,
replete so long;
but what will fill this space,
this voided aching place?

The womb once full
is now an empty sphere;
its tenant gone,
its surface slack, as
at the ocean's edge
we'd find the same appears:

where grainy sands lie flat
along a heavy beach,
new mounds are moved
to moon's magnetic reach

and feathered fingers
of the sea's firm hand
form rigid ripples
on the sculpted sand.

Now close the circuit
in this vacuum—
free the current
make it flow—
bridge the vacant gap
from womb to aching breast—
and put the child to suck.

Root Stock

The stem of me
like a stream
feeds the growth
and forms the plant,
shapes and
nourishes each petal
to its full bloom.

I proudly
lift the arms of me
to frame
this product
of my life,

and passersby
not knowing,
comment
on the
brilliant flower
that they see.

Morning Prayers

The living waters
fill me with a
soft and gentle current
flowing over rocks
rippling past the stones
to Peace.

The *Shoheyn Ad* washes
like soft rain
across the parched desert
fills my soul
and gives me Peace.

The pure melody
floats around me
while words of *Eyl Adon*
praising all of God's Creation
bring me Peace.

Lift me on waves
of *she'kinah*
rock my soul
and soothe me with
this *Shabbat* Peace.

The Dawn of Time;
all the vast expanse
of the Firmament
are open to my inner eye
as I drink in Peace.

My voice joins yours
in the *Modim*
and again in *Sim Shalom*
as we thank our Creator
for this moment of
pure Peace.

*In this I name the prayers that are read during the Saturday
morning service:*

Sholheyn Ad	Abiding Spirit
El Adon	God is Lord
She'kinah	Spirit of God
Modim	Prayer of Thanks
Sim Shalom	Prayer for Peace

Kaddish for a Friend

I take you from the water's edge
and show you groves of trees.
We move in cadence with *Shabbat*,
and we are one.

I take you from the azure sea
and show you my retreat.
We sit in silent prayer,
and we are one.

I take you from the lonely shore
and show you my new friends.
We get to know their names,
and we are one.

I take you from your lonely grave
and hold you in my heart.
We share the *She'kinah*,
and we are one.

from the Hebrew—Kaddish: Mourner's prayer
She'kinah: Holy Spirit

Lake Effect

Fractured crystals sparkle down
from clear blue sunlit skies
lacy hexahedrons fall
across the canvas of my eyes.
Snow? no, not at all:
    it's Lake Effect.

Heavy metal pewter gray
pressed tight, stretched
across the day's horizon;
is this a portent of
a nasty storm?
    No: Lake Effect.

Fog-wrapped morning,
chill and dreary,
don't despair
the day bodes fair;
afternoon, around the corner,
finds a day quite warm and sunny.
    Lake Effect.

Thunder rolls across the sky,
lightning blooms on far horizons
earth lies flat and begs for rain,
heavens won't release their burden:
    Lake Effect.

Day on day, it goes this way:
    Lake Effect.

The Pool

I love the old women
who come from Morningside
to swim in McCann's pool.
They wear their caps, their suits
and goggles as a badge.
They're long and lean
with short salt-cured do's, they're
walnut where their suits don't shade,
beach babies all their lives with
sand in their shoes.

Trained to swim against the tides
at Morningside,
their *crawl* cuts splashless
through the water,
breast is sleek as seals, and
bunny in the basket's strong enough
to bring a wayward swimmer
back to shore.

When they come to the pool
you know the Sound's gone
down past 62°, and
it's just a tad too cool
down at the shore.

On the Beach

Splash on the rosy hues of dawn,
    the birth of new and soft
        and growing things.
Add the colors of a day;
    the morning patterns won't be stilled
        as stippled dapples move across the sky, and
    vagrant breezes shift the scene set in my frame.

Paint high noon brilliant gold;
    an all-pervading sun eliminates the shadows
        and puts all life in clear relief.
There shines through every cherished image
        laser beams of truth; my composition's set
    a timeless bubble frozen in its place.

A clear blue wash tints
    the hours of the afternoon
        and alters every hour with a deeper tone;
    it is an quiet time
        when grass reflects the sky.

Look back and see what I have done, and
    purple sundown is the crucial test.
        If I've accomplished all the tasks
    I've set myself to do, I am content
        to be enfolded in the deep envelope of night.

Interlude

There is no time
so quiet as
a twilight on the sound.

The gulls fly high;
time to deny
their normal feeding ground.

The crowd is gone;
their footprints filled
and essence washed away.

The boats sit low
while wind is stilled,
so ends another day.

The Seashore

I lie silent
watch and wonder;
I lie heavy
time to ponder.

Were I to create this scene,
would tides obey the moon's command?
Would I keep the ocean green
count each grain of sand?

Would I know to shape the fin
on every special little fish,
give each hermit crab
an empty shell to fill his wish?

Would the grasses stand so tall,
each blade set out to catch the breeze,
as the water sloshes through
changing patterns in the frieze?

I lie quiet, dreaming
till the sun sets in the west;
watching as the day goes by,
I am the seashore, gone to rest.

Ecosystem

There lies in the west, a land
           all wind-swept clean and ocean-wide
     called the *Pastures of the Lord.*

There owl and dog,
           small snake and bug,
     make their home in grassy boles.

There symbiotic Indian
           lived and died
     and never left a mark.

One with nature,
           God's companion,
     moved in rhythm with his world.

Life-giving savage, he
           burned the brush
     and fed the soil,

planted small food
           in the grassland,
     not to move the roots.

Beast of prey,
           he faced the wind,
     set his footsteps in the furrows,

paced his pathway
>   in the grasses,
>   took his needs and left the rest.

Dead, he hung high on his platform,
>   fed his friends
>   and left the prairie clean.

I, The Song

I am the Song of God's creation
the rocks, the sea, the sky and me.
My chord was set
at time's inception
note on note to blend with nature.

I keep my song,
strong and sure,
against the stillness of the rocks,
as they hold firm
beneath my feet.

I sound my song,
clean, clear notes,
with tumbling waters
as they wash out to the
vast eternal sea.

I sing my song,
sweet honeyed notes,
against the silence of the sky
as it flows to the endless
span of heaven.

When my harmony is true,
balanced with the rest of nature,
I live my melody
as it was intended.
I walk with beauty,

I, the song.

About Time

time is a magic thing
it flows, it stops at will, or
carries us along
its ineffable journey
minute by minute
day by day
unchanged by whim
unmoved by our command

The Hour Glass

I was born into this life
with my internal clock
ticking away the hours
and the minutes of my days.
I am aware of time;
its essence is with me all ways;
it is the measured beat
that frames my days.

It is 10 a.m. whether I'm at business,
or shopping, or waiting for a bus;
three o'clock feels the same on a busy day
as it does on a loosely quiet day;
my personal activity has no bearing
on the flow of sand
within my frozen glass of time;
my days are numbered and my hours set.

Each minute that I use is registered
somewhere in the ledger of my life;
let me use them well;
I'll not wish them gone
nor wish them back again;
each one is precious,
each one has a value all its own,
each one is mine and bears my name.

Priorities

My days are crowded close
with work and dreams.

What shall I do,
how shall I use my hours?

If I'm to take the time to dream
the work must go undone,

if I finish all my tasks
the songs must go unsung.

The Clock

I circle through
the hours of my life
the minutes tick and tocking
through my day.

Each day a step along
the path I follow;
each hour just a dream
that's told along the way.

The hands click past each mark;
there is no other now or then,
no one to answer to my
question: *when?*

I set my steps to walk
the predetermined path
that runs straight through
to my predestined end.

The Sundial

sun shines—
lovely light
across my face
measuring the hours

rain falls—
footsteps patter
on my surface
marking off the minutes

clouds gather—
moving bars of dark
across the sun, and
time's held captive

erratic minutes
here, then gone
while I lie quiet
in the shadow

moonrise—
lovely, lucid
glow, too soft
to make its mark

holds my hand
still, as I dream
of sunny hours
in the garden.

The End of the Time Zone

Seven a.m. comes hard
on a winter day in Milan.

The air hangs quiet,
chilled and dark;
the moon and stars
still rule, with dawn
another hour away.

The bed is soft, warm,
filled with dreams;
breakfast doesn't beckon
till eight o'clock or so.
There are chores
that wait, and
duties that won't hold
while sun comes slow
across the endless plains.

My clock's awry
tilted out of true;
morning moves in late, and
evenings never end.

Seven a.m. comes hard in Milan.
Michigan, that is.

7:10 a.m.

In *the nautical twilight of dawn,*
    that magic moment just before daybreak,
there is a fluid quality
    to the light and air,

An all-pervading gleam
    shines dull across the scene,
and artificial lights glow pale
    in the dim wash that precedes the day.

The sea lies flat and mirrors back
    the black and endless image of the sky;
birds inhale, and trees
    embrace the clouds of night.

Like statues, small creatures stand entranced,
    en route from hole to hunt,
involuntary tweaks and twitches
    betray the life of them.

The morning sun repaints
    the picture of the night; those
small steles move, then scurry to the hunt
    or, in a flurry, vanish back to shadow.

Another day has come.

Time Line

I was seven when
they bombed Hawaii,
and eleven when
that war ended.

When I was seventeen,
they sent my dates
to fight their battles in Pusan
and Pyanyang.

When my babies
learned their A B C's,
they were taught
Atom, Bomb, and Cuba.

I had my third child
while the Nation mourned
for Kennedy, then
King was killed.

When my daughters
wanted cartoons,
TV fed them, instead,
live scenes from Vietnam.

My husband's 70th
birthday was marked
by our first
attack on Iraq.

On nine-eleven,
when we gave our newest
baby her first bath,
we watched in horror
as the towers fell
hour after hour on TV.

Enough, I say, *dayenu*,
give us peace.

Excuses

When winter's come
and all is glum
I have no heart
    to work,

when it is spring
and everything's
in bloom, I just won't go
    to work,

when summer's here
blue skies are clear
the breezes bid me not
    to work,

and in the fall
the leaves and all
keep me too enthralled
    to work.

I swore that I'd allot
a quarter of the clock
ten hours of a week
    to work

but find with all
my time on call
I have no time
    to work.

So I'll write
and if it's trite
it's best I do not say
    it's work.

Time Out—01/01/01

As I sat and wrote my checks
and dated them 01/01/01, I
felt I'd entered *cybernestion*
and now was writing code.
I wondered was it good, or
was there a sinister complexion?

Remembered last year,
when computers were reset, so
as they came to finish 1999,
they would not roll back,
erase a thousand years of ledger,
and place us in the past—
at 1 and 0, 0, 0.

Now, this year when we changed
our number-speak
to satisfy this exquisite
deus ex machination,
we went from 42K *to MMI* so
there would be no more confusion.

If this is so, will it know
to progress through this year
in cadence
01-, 02-, 03-, and onward
through the pages;
and will it know to roll it-
self back in its future sequence
to 01/01/02?

Time Was

I watch in memory
a scene from long ago
when trees were tall
and full of leaves
and flowers filled the field.

I hear in memory
the music of this day,
humming bees and tapping feet
and children singing
at their play.

I smell the day
all green and new;
the soft sweet grass
and sneakers squeaking
on warm clay.

I feel again the day
deep within my bones,
youth's untried strength
and vibrant dreams
of destiny.

Mirror Image

A glance in the mirror, but what is that
the face is full, the jaw is slack;

where is the girl I am inside,
where is the girl who was a bride;

my eyes have dimmed, my vision's blurred,
my ears are muffled, words are slurred;

the music that I loved so well,
I hear the brass, can't hear the bells;

the feet that sped take slower steps,
the hands, once skilled, are not adept;

the drums I hear now down the hall,
the music coming through the walls,
are fading fast.

To Youth

Let me see with your eyes,
see the trees and the skies
and watch the day unfold.
Let me see with young eyes
for mine are growing old.

Let me hear with your ears,
hear laughter and cheers
and listen to tales that are told.
Let me hear with young ears
for mine are growing old.

Block in the scene
with strokes bold and strong;
splash on rich colors
write new words to old songs.

Let me feel as you feel
experience, new and intense,
the thrill of the promise of life.
Let me be young at heart
for mine is growing old.

About the Author

Ms Rubin retired from a technical writing career in 1999. It was then she found her voice as Devorah. She has published three chapbooks: *Song of the Bee*, in 2000, *Sabbath Journey*, in 2002, and *Love Notes*, in 2003. Devorah has taught workshops in chapbook design and poetry for seniors and is active in several poetry associations, local and national. Her work with the Stratford Clergy has been staged in The Holocaust Memorial programs they produce annually. This year she realizes her goal of having her first full-length book of poetry published. Her work has been read from *The Green Room* in San Diego; *Crazy Wisdom* in Ann Arbor; and various workshops in Connecticut, including *Live at Ives* in New Haven, which sessions were later broadcast on CT-T.V.

www.ingramcontent.com/pod-product-compliance
Lightning Source LLC
LaVergne TN
LVHW091157080426
835509LV00006B/735